# After After-Thoughts

# York Van Nixon III

Nex Millennium Press

Washington, D.C. 20001

Copyright © 2025 by York Van Nixon III

ISBN: 979-8-9936610-1-8

BISAC: POE023000 POETRY / Subjects & Themes / General

All rights reserved. No part of this book may be reproduced in any form, including information storage and retrieval systems, without written permission from the publisher or author, except for review.

[Cover design and corresponding images created by Courtni Wright]

This collection of thoughts is dedicated to my son, York Van Nixon IV, my trusted inspiration.

ALSO BY YORK VAN NIXON III

Novels
Missing Steps
Alternative Acts
A Sparrow Hawk Loves Yew

Short Stories
Souls Over The Hill

Poetry
Songs Aging Sing After
After-Thoughts

## Table of Contents

Foreword .................................................................................... vii
Primal Scream Again............................................................... 1
Ahead the Moon ....................................................................... 3
As Day Abeds ........................................................................... 7
Til Crocus Crow ....................................................................... 9
Gloam Fore Light..................................................................... 11
Late Blooms ............................................................................. 13
After the Gloam ....................................................................... 17
Spring Come Showers ............................................................. 21
Night Tag.................................................................................. 25
Dal-Lea ..................................................................................... 29
Beads of Late Summer ............................................................ 33
Between Candles ..................................................................... 37
Not Waiting to Exhale ............................................................ 43
Fore First Drop ........................................................................ 47
Missing Steps ........................................................................... 51
Time Machine.......................................................................... 57
My Familiar.............................................................................. 61
One-Only-One II...................................................................... 67
The Tattered-Tale Heart ......................................................... 73
A Nutmeg Kiss......................................................................... 79
Home in Loam ......................................................................... 83
Curling Fingers ........................................................................ 93
Rays of a Son............................................................................ 99
Fires of Mt. Erato..................................................................... 105
No Help Wanted ..................................................................... 111

Past Event Horizons .................................................................................... 117
Walking on Water......................................................................................... 121
Your Bad........................................................................................................ 125
Early in the City ........................................................................................... 127
A Cheap Vacation......................................................................................... 129

# Foreword

## After After-Thoughts

In *After After-Thoughts*, York Van Nixon III gathers the residue of time—what remains after the storm, after the bloom, after the breath—and renders it luminous. Each poem inhabits that fragile space between exhale and inhale, where silence hums with the memory of sound and existence reconsiders its shape.

The collection unfolds like a spiral rather than a line, echoing its title's recursion. Nixon's voice travels through elemental cycles—birth, decay, return—revealing that the "after" is never an ending, but a reawakening. The womb becomes water, the breath becomes drumbeat, and even the ashes of memory whisper their way back into light.

Across these pages, time is not an arrow but a tide. It folds upon itself in poems such as *Primal Scream Again*, where creation is both beginning and echo; *Ahead the Moon*, where mortality bends toward grace; and *Late Blooms*, where age flowers defiantly against dusk. The poems breathe as one continuum, each stanza a pulse in the body of the eternal.

Van Nixon's language is sculpted from music, dance and meditation. He fuses modern awareness with ancient rhythm—African, spiritual, cosmic. His syntax drifts between the corporeal and the celestial, weaving sound into silence, and silence into revelation. Every metaphor becomes a reflection: of ancestry, of art, of the soul's persistence through time's dissolving frame.

There is grief here, yes—but it is the fertile grief of transformation. Each image, whether it be a trembling petal or a sigh between lovers, is reborn in the next line, transfigured yet familiar. To read these poems is

to step inside a continuous breath—to inhabit the stillness that precedes creation and follows remembrance.

In *After After-Thoughts*, York Van Nixon III invites us to dwell not in the beginning or the end, but in the shimmering threshold between. It is there—in the hum before words, in the silence after song—that we find the eternal rhythm of being.

*After After-Thoughts*

*After After-Thoughts*

# Primal Scream Again

Let me lie between the silence of seconds
Reposing in the womb of warm waters
Tethering an Innie to an Outie, within
Possibilities of circular time

Echoes ripple across membranes unseen,
Drums of the body beat in dark cadence,
A whispered tremor of breath becoming form,
Cradled in the velvet hush of return.

Before speech, there was the trembling hum,
Before thought, a glimmer of formless light,
Arcs of energy seeking their mirror,
The self folding inward, then outward again.

No clock here ticks with cruel indifference,
No hand pushes the hours to their grave;
Only the swell of pulse within tide,
A round of beginnings refusing to end.

Mothered by waters that cannot break,
Fathered by silence too deep to name,
I drift between the bone and the ether,
Hearing the birth cry not yet released.

Each second births another second,
Unclasping into spirals of forever;
Time unthreads itself into soft fibers,
Winding me back to what never was lost.

The scream waits, like lightning in the marrow,
Ready to tear the shroud of serenity;
Yet even storm becomes lullaby here,
Each thunderclap a hand rocking the void.

What am I but a circle's echo,
A skin stretched tight on timeless drums?
Let me remain within this folding,
Neither first nor last, but ever again.

*After After-Thoughts*

*After After-Thoughts*

# Ahead the Moon

Lonely last to bloom
Early bask in twilight
Warily, fore night soon
Reject yon unending sleep

Weep not your erred augur
Life but infinite spokes
Heralding round a wheel
Til rungs of iron peal

Silver hush of dusk descends,
Echoes ripple through the air,
Each pulse a whispered promise
That nothing ends, but bends.

Crickets tune their brittle strings,
The owl rehearses her decree,
Dreams awaken under cover,
Softly woven, deft, unseen.

Petals shiver in their dew,
Afraid to bow or break again,
Yet moonlight strokes their trembling hue,
And names them not in vain.

Ahead, the moon ascends her chair,
A matron draped in argent lace,
Her fingers tracing mortal cares
Across the somber face of space.

She hums of stars that came and went,
Of tides that kissed and turned away,
Of hearts that burned through firmament
To meet the dawn's delayed decay.

*After After-Thoughts*

No end, she murmurs, but return,
A cycle wrought of ache and grace,
For even ashes twist and yearn
To find their rightful place.

And so, though night may veil your eyes,
And silence weigh the soul within,
Ahead the moon, still steadfast, lies—
Rebuking death, recalling kin.

Sleep, if you must, but not too deep,
For waking's but a mirrored tune,
And every bloom the dark may keep
Still leans— ahead the moon.

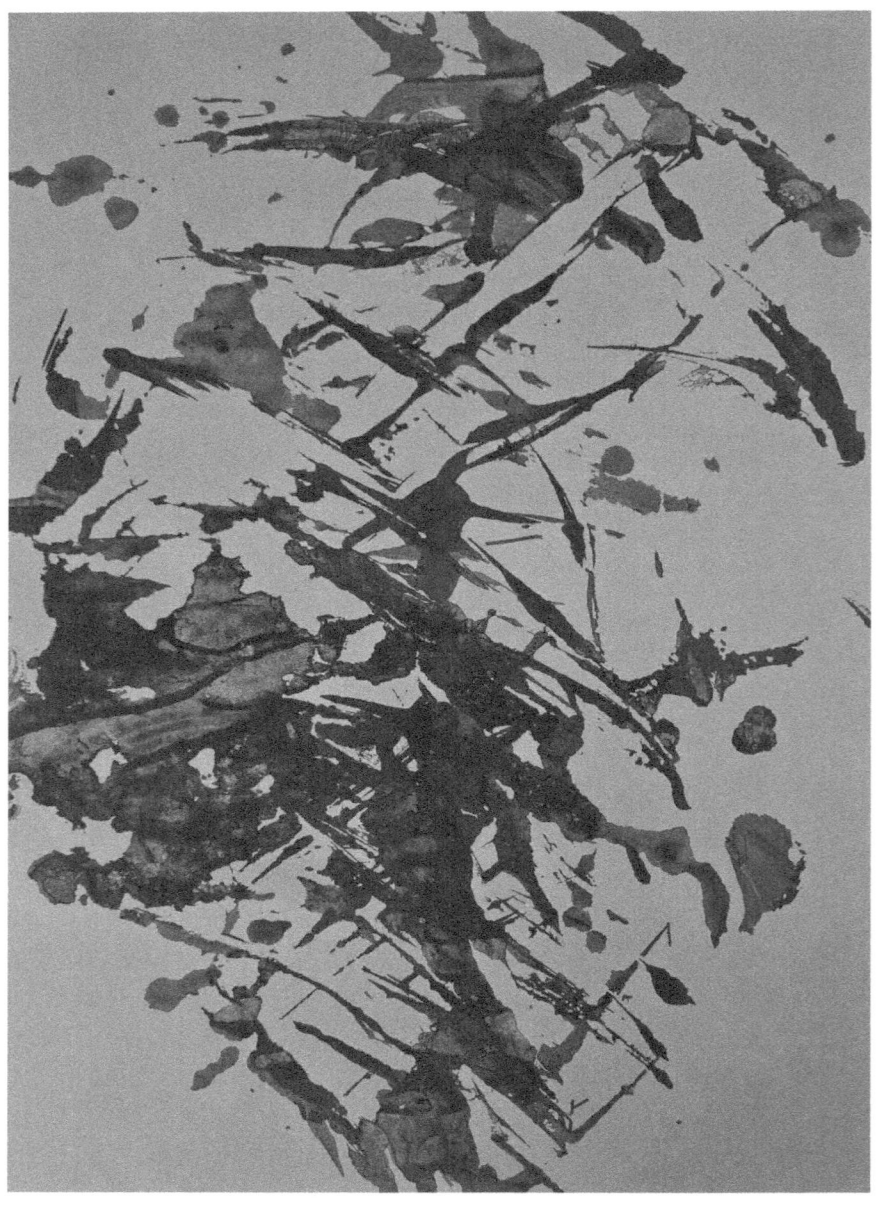

# As Day Abeds

Rays of Summer's aurora
fade with each zephyr's gasp
calling winged heralds
gliding on warm currents
to gardens below our horizons
where robins wait to sing
yet, the approaching silence
will never leave me without song
rhythms of the heart await
melodies of two beating as one,
the sound of one clapping against
warm palms of aged thoughts,
storied memories free of time

*After After-Thoughts*

# Til Crocus Crow

Autumn colored pages
Leaf from my calendar
And Fall onto drifts
Of Winter's indolent kiss

Her plump red lips
Belie a gelid heart
Devoid of Spring's
Passioned green cheek

As my bent pen dries
Of inflamed ink and dew
A wrinkled face smiles
From the bottom well

No need for a bucket
Echoes replace drops
Tears with silent plops
To wet this parched mouth

*After After-Thoughts*

*After After-Thoughts*

# Gloam Fore Light

Moments before hint of dawn
Consciousness emerged
Within a familiar dream
Usual pains replaced by
A forgotten option to enjoy
Moment without the penumbra
Of variegated pharmaceuticals
No need for a sip of bedstand water
To flush chemicals. Forget concerns
About prescribed dilatory actions
Accumulating in subcutaneous pieces of
Flesh vying for the brass ring
Awarded to a patient mortician
In essence, my body ceases to be
It is now there as a post thought
Instead of every heartbeat
Before a cacophony of synapses
I think therefore now and then

## Late Blooms

Soon last to bloom
Late morning child
Spring came too soon
Suckling baby on air

Browned wrinkled teats
Tease chapped dry lips
Crying for mother
Soured breasts

At parting hour
No sure embrace
Just soiled sheets
Self-image incomplete

Before robins sing
After nightingales pine
As snapdragons flame
Late bloomers sigh

As if Winter's kiss
Licked their feet
Cry for milk
Die for life

Shooting for sun
Way past midnight
Well late into
Prime of life

Ashes of dreams
Smolder beneath rain
The scent of loss
Still sweet with pain

*After After-Thoughts*

Petals unfold
In defiant grace
Veins like rivers
On weathered face

Roots clutch clay
Older than tears
Whispering softly
Through buried years

The harvest waits
For trembling hands
Fruits too tender
For rough commands

A cracked mirror hums
With gentle deceit
Reflecting the youth
Time failed to repeat

Still stems rise
From composted sorrow
Breathing out hope
For one more tomorrow

When evening falls
And lilacs sleep
Old hearts remember
The vows they keep

Soon last to bloom
Late evening child
Spring comes again
To reconcile

*After After-Thoughts*

# After the Gloam

Tis Fall, when leaves drift beyond sight,
burnished and brittle in the rearview's gleam.
Summer's warmth recedes beneath the skin,
its echo a hum before the gloam.

Maple, birch, dogwood, elm, and cedar
loosen their grip on air and memory.
The wind carries what cannot be kept—
the scent of ash, the murmur of returning.

We say hello as we say goodbye,

hands brushing against invisible glass.
Ideas awaken where silence sleeps,
an infant thought taking its first breath of air.

Twilight leans against the horizon's edge,
a thin silver mist curling between day and dream.
Fireflies gather their faint electricity,
as if time itself has begun to flicker.

The night exhales its patient smoke.
Voices drift from unseen corners,
each one uncertain whether it is prayer or song,
and every word dissolves before it lands.

Beneath the firs, the ground listens.
Roots tremble with remembered rain.
Somewhere, a cry pierces the cool—
not grief, but the ache of renewal.

Earth Mother closes her arms around the soil.
The sky folds its pale fabric.
The Father's breath hesitates,
then drifts toward another morning.

*After After-Thoughts*

The moon hums low over a shallow pond.
Water answers in broken syllables.
Reeds bend without reason or remorse,
their motion an old conversation continued.

A stillness gathers where sound once lived.
Owls call, not to hunt, but to be heard.
Their wings erase what the stars confess.
Distance feels nearer than thought.

A field lies open—grain without gold,
the air scented with iron and root.
Every stalk bends to a rhythm older
than the names we gave it.

In the haze, the outline of a child—
not born, but waiting—
traces a circle in the dust.
Even the shadows pause to watch.

The wind carries voices from nowhere,
each vowel drawn thin with longing.
They do not end. They do not begin.
They hover between breath and belief.

Light arrives shyly through the trees,
uncertain of its purpose.
It lingers on dew, on the curve of a stone,
and finds the world still breathing.

*After After-Thoughts*

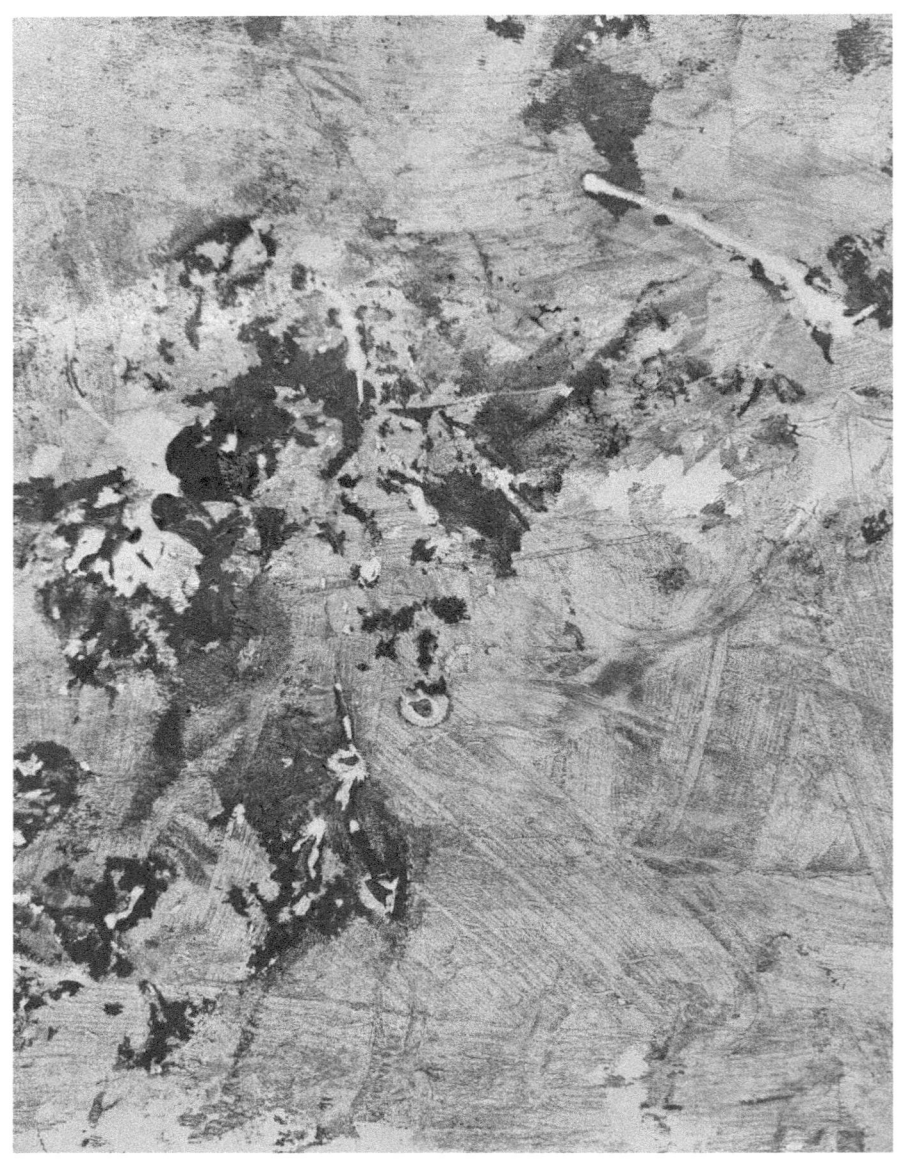

# Spring Come Showers

YES,
Distant thunder reminds me—
Of nights when we were embers,
Burning blue upon the pillows,
The sheets surrendering all dryness,
Our mouths still searching breath.

The walls kept count of sighs,
Bedposts hummed their low confessions,
A fan turned secrets into wind—
Whirling, whooshing, tasting skin,
Each curve a map of warmth
Drawn by evaporating desire.

The lightning painted us briefly—
A fresco of shadow and gleam.
Your shoulder glowed like prophecy,
Your lips, an unanswered prayer.
Between each flash we vanished,
Only to be reborn in touch.

Outside, the storm rehearsed its hunger,
Clouds swelling with their ache.
Rain pressed its mouth to glass—
Kissing, retreating, returning again—
The rhythm of something ancient
That the body remembers first.

Your scent rose—musk and rainfall,
A sweetness grown from heat.
My fingers traced the memory
Of where your pulse had slept.
The air was thick with promise,
Heavy, holy, and near.

*After After-Thoughts*

Our laughter slipped between thunderclaps,
Soft lightning beneath the tongue.
The night grew lush, forgiving,
A slow descent through dreams—
Where even silence dared to sing,
And every breath was answered.

The fan kept time like a drum,
The window shivered in applause.
Branches bowed their wet applause,
While thunder, jealous, rolled below—
A basso prayer for union,
A hymn of storm and skin.

Your hair, a constellation of night,
Held sparks from the storm's own heart.
I gathered them in trembling hands
As if they might still glow for me—
Little embers of remembrance,
Each one whispering stay.

When the rain at last surrendered,
The room exhaled its heat.
Sheets lay limp as flowers,
Spent petals on the floor.
We drifted past exhaustion,
Into that grace called still.

Moonlight stitched us quietly—
Threading pale silver through the dark.
Your back curved like shoreline sand,
Your sigh receded with the tide.
In the hush between heartbeats,
Love folded into rest.

*After After-Thoughts*

Yet even then, the air remembered.
Each droplet carried your echo,
Each gust your half-formed name.
I lay awake inside the scent
Of what the night had written—
A psalm of wet devotion.

Dawn crept barefoot through the curtains,
Her hands cupped full of light.
She kissed the rain from my eyelids,
And brushed the dream aside.
Still, I heard the thunder murmur—
Your voice beneath the sky.

So let Spring come with her showers,
With her fevered, fragrant touch.
Let her find the corners of us
That winter could not reach.
Let her baptize our quiet longing
And turn it once more to bloom.

For love, like rain, is patient—
Falling where it's needed most.
It gathers in forgotten hollows,
Seeps through stone and doubt.
And when the storm is over,
The earth remembers how to breathe

*After After-Thoughts*

# Night Tag

Late glimmers of afternoon:
Aging children play tag past twilight.
Calls to playmates long gone home to sleep.
Awake in dreams. School bells pealing rain.
I see you hiding behind a shadow.
Tomorrow I may be "it". Or now.

Fallow holes await dust.
Clocks shedding time filling urns.
White carnations ready to bloom.
It's your turn. Promise not to tell.
Mother's calling. Dinner's getting cold.
"No dessert!" No sweets for cold lips.
Just soft organ hymns for lullabies.

Sleep forever in a single bed.
Remember all. See everything.
Eyes wide—shut—abrupt.
No snores wake you up.
Quiet tattle-tell-heart.
Skipped the last beat.
Recall when you wished upon a star.
Just the one that came true.

Streetlamps flicker like old eyes blinking.
Their yellow hum remembers laughter.
Sidewalk chalk fades into mist.
The hopscotch grid now graveyard geometry.
Each square a box of waiting names.
Even the moon counts softly—"one, two, three."

*After After-Thoughts*

Tag again, in secret.
The ghost child runs the alley of your thought.
You reach, but your hand meets vapor.
Warm air, scented of cut grass and dusk.
He whispers your name backward.
You almost answer, but forget your tongue.

Dew collects on sneakers.
No one left to chase.
A breath, half sigh, half prayer.
Dusty marbles roll beneath a maple root.
Lightning bugs blink Morse for farewell.
The tree hums the alphabet of loss.

In attic trunks, the rules remain.
Folded paper, rubber bands, and dares.
A list of who was last "it."
Their names now written in obituaries.
Childhood plays long games.
No one wins, only remembers.

Rain begins softly, as if afraid to wake.
Roof gutters hum lullabies of the gone.
Sheets pulled up to chin—pretend it's warmth.
Dreams smell of mud and Sunday shoes.
Somewhere, a bell rings three times.
Or maybe it's your pulse, trying again.

Shadow-tag at midnight.
The mirror blinks and turns away.
Windows fog with unspoken names.
The house creaks its old refrain:
"Ready or not…"
No one replies.

*After After-Thoughts*

Time hides in corners, too.
Under beds, behind curtains of light.
It waits for its cue, patient as dust.
One child always forgets to run.
Another never stops counting.
The game begins again.

In dreams, you find your teammates.
They glow faint as candle wicks.
Each face a clock without hands.
You call their names—echoes only.
Yet someone giggles, far off, near dawn.
You chase the sound, barefoot through rain.

Footprints fade like breath on glass.
Still, you follow—always "it."
No turning back toward the porch light.
The door is locked, the key dissolved.
Your shadow races ahead.
It never tires. It never hides.

Morning mist erases the field.
The bell rings once—no class, no roll call.
Just wind marking attendance.
The world yawns, unaware you're still playing.
Heaven's recess has no whistle.
Only silence, passing for peace.

Somewhere, a mother calls again.
Her voice a hymn, her face the sun.
You run toward it, laughing,
Hands open, ready to tag eternity.
All the others wait their turn.
No one ever says "Game over."

*After After-Thoughts*

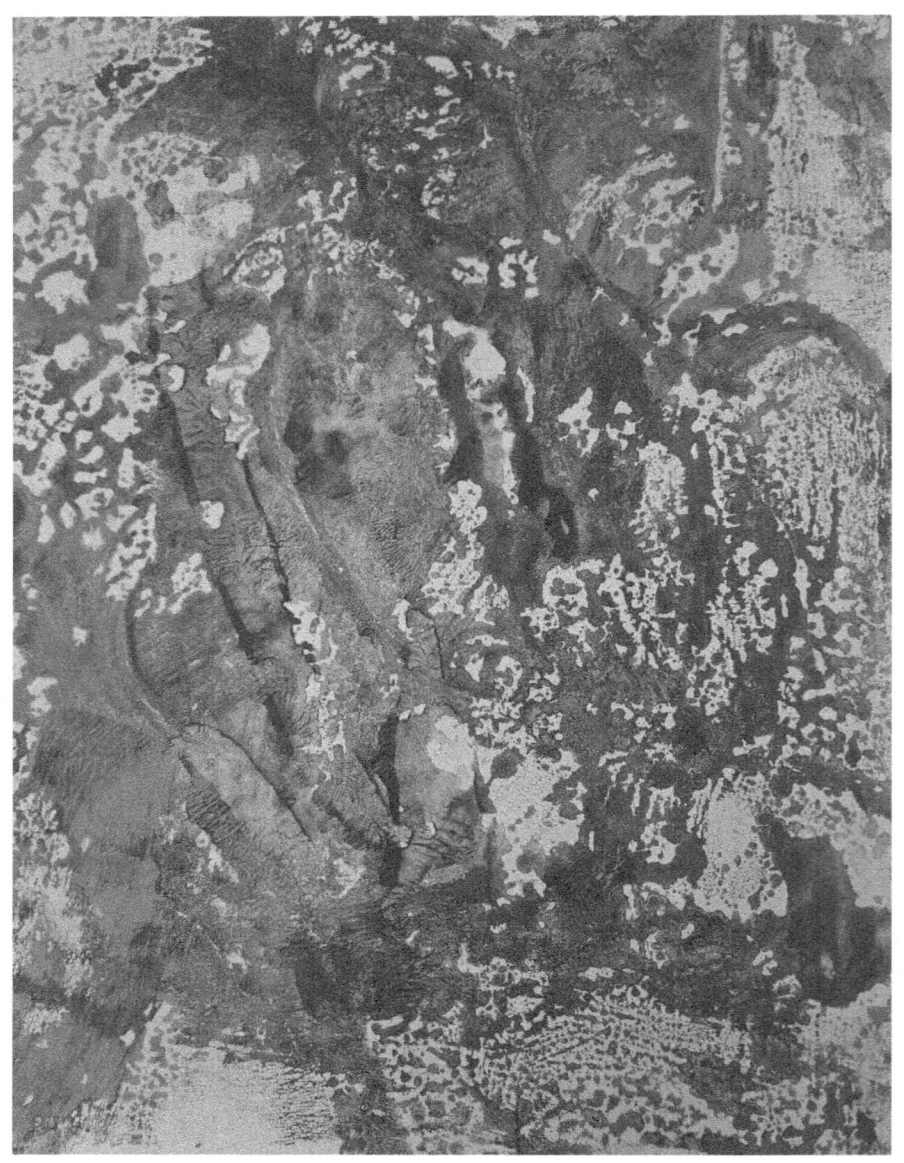

# Dal-Lea

A cawing crow dines on dreams and marrow,
while a decaying corpse has a nightmare of hope.

Somewhere, a gossamer door is ajar between two separate worlds;
the dimension of this universe is in singularity's peril.
Morning slips into darkness midday

as flowers close their petals in fear of the dark;
rivers change direction while the desert is wet.
tears stream to heaven, from the mountains instead.
Halfway through your dream, you realize the truth—
imagination is the pathway to the first step of success.
Demons, goblins and fire-licking doom are just passing clouds,
providing you believe in yourself and wake up soon.

Now the sun melts clocks upon the bones of time,
and the hourglass inhales your sighs.
The wind paints hieroglyphs across your skin,
telling stories of when you were water.

Angels crouch upon telephone wires,
whispering numbers that add up to infinity.
Each equation bends toward longing,
each sum dissolves into the sea.

In the field of the mind, cows are crows,
their hooves black feathers that scatter thought.
They dine on the marrow of memory,
chewing shadows until they sing.

*After After-Thoughts*

A rose-colored storm folds into itself,
and the sky becomes an eyelid of glass.
Stars drip like candle wax,
and each drop burns through the dream of night.

Your mother's lullaby echoes backward,
a cradle swinging in reverse.
Even birth seems a kind of farewell—
a ribbon cut before the gift is known.

Oceans breathe like sleeping beasts,
their salt the taste of ancient grief.
Somewhere beneath the foam,
a clockfish swallows a pearl of time.

In the orchard of bones, fruit glows blue.
Each bite is a whisper: *remember me.*
You chew eternity down to seed,
and plant it where thought begins.

A mirror reflects the part of you that forgot to exist.
It bows, bends, shatters—then reforms as light.
You are the glass, the fracture, the flame,
and the dust dancing between them.

The moon drinks deeply from your veins,
turning your sleep to silver milk.
Dreams bloom like fungi on forgotten prayers,
soft and glowing in the cave of your skull.

Dawn hesitates on the edge of reason,
afraid to wake the gods of dust.

*After After-Thoughts*

But even gods must dream of us—
for what is creation, if not return?

So rise, child of crows and cows and clockless suns;
walk barefoot through the marrow of your mind.
The gossamer door swings wide once more,
and every nightmare opens into art.

## *Beads of Late Summer*

Hues of ebbing summers
imbue my eyes—
cascading rias,
timpani without batons.

Over my sunburned shoulder,
footprints fade with the tide.
Each step a lighter echo
of what desire once weighed.

The air trembles—
reeds bow under their own hush.
A bee drifts past, slow as thought.
Amber settles in the shallows.

Dragonflies hover
like fragments of mirrors.
Their wings hum the perimeter
of a vanishing noon.

A sail crosses the bay—
white cloth, bone, breath—
a gesture that remembers wind
but no longer chases it.

Cicadas beat time
against the skin of dusk.
Laughter unravels
somewhere inland.

*After After-Thoughts*

I stand at the edge,
grain by grain dissolving.
Between pulse and tide
the self grows porous.

The sun reclines,
its light thinning into honey.
Evening gathers the world
in lavender and hush.

The tide speaks in broken vowels,
a grammar older than grief.
Each wave returns changed,
unable to explain its journey.

Now shadows open
like pages unread.
Stillness writes its answer
in the body's salt.

I listen.
Not for meaning—
for what remains
after sound.

The beads of summer glisten
in the mind's last warmth—
a necklace unstrung,
its shimmer becoming air.

## Between Candles

thanks from all,
aging children
apart the serenity
of a copious womb,

giving all
and asking
nothing in return
adrift

since a primal scream
without life-giving tether
we are sated
by bounties

imbued with
warm reflections
within the hearts
and minds

of family
and cherished friends,
the cosmic dust of
immortality

whispered prayers
between candles
burning low
and rising smoke

*After After-Thoughts*

each spark
a name recalled
each tear
a mirror of grace

we walk
toward the hush
of our own
becoming

no haste
no final word
only breath
circling breath

in twilight's
folded hands
time gathers
its children

between candles
and shadows' drift
our laughter
flickers still

a gesture,
a sigh,
a kindness
left behind

the pulse of stars
measures our hearts
their rhythm
never lost

*After After-Thoughts*

we dream
inside the dark
until morning

leans close

memory's tide
lapping gently
over the ruins
of yesterday

love endures
like marrow's hymn
singing softly
to the bone

each life
a trembling note
in an unseen
chorale

the womb of sky
cradles us again
returning
what we borrowed

every ending
is a slow light
folding back
into creation

we rest
in radiant dust
unashamed
of vanishing

*After After-Thoughts*

and somewhere
a child laughs
unaware
of time's decree

the circle
tightens kindly
holding nothing
and all

we stand
between candles
neither flame
nor smoke

but breath
made visible
through
gratitude

the silence hums
a living chord
as stars
descend in prayer

and love
remains unnamed
yet wholly
ours.

*After After-Thoughts*

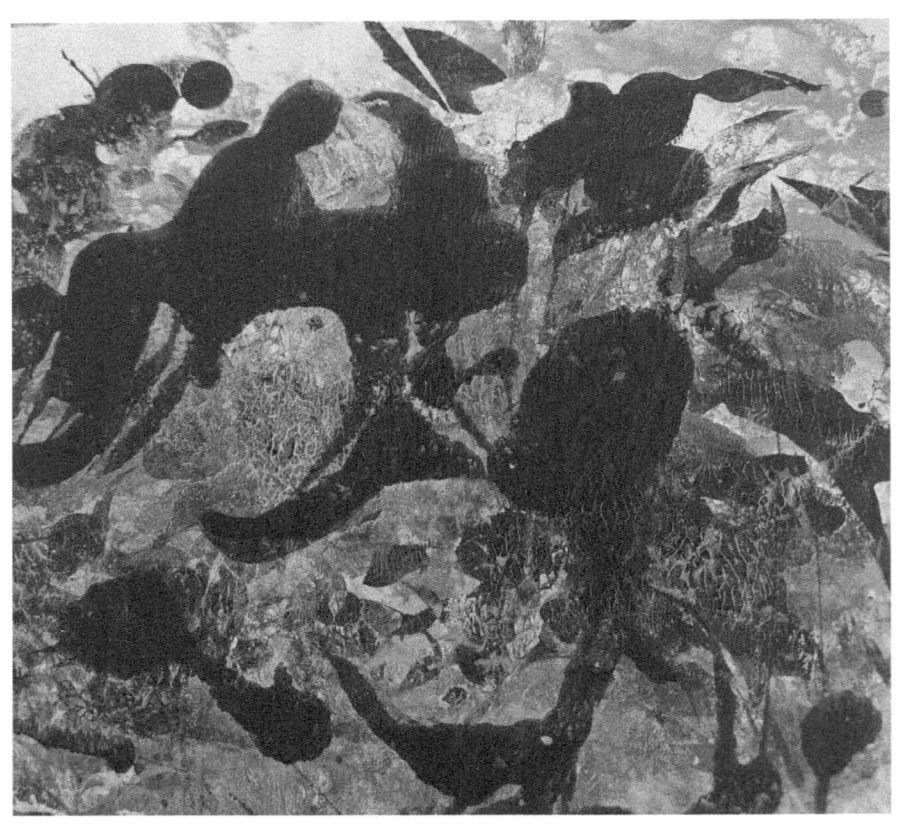

*After After-Thoughts*

# Not Waiting to Exhale

Change is the honey of life
Dawns drip bands of possibilities
An eternity existing between breaths
Foreshadowing an ongoing nexus

The moment before the inhale hums,
A pregnant stillness sweet and aching,
As if the universe itself pauses
To taste its own becoming.

Light uncoils from shadow's cocoon,
Golden threads through unseen hands;
Each shimmer a promise, a pulse,
A map drawn upon the mist.

We are not waiting, only weaving—
Between what was dreamt and what unfolds;
Every heartbeat a subtle rebellion
Against the myth of permanence.

Exhale, and the world reforms,
Petal by petal, breath by breath;
The air carries our metamorphosis
Like pollen searching for new bloom.

Even silence speaks in tremors,
Vibrations of things not yet named;
The void is fertile, the pause electric,
Holding galaxies in embryo.

What dies becomes foundation,
What slips away becomes song;
Loss is merely translation
From form to frequency to flame.

*After After-Thoughts*

Change drinks from its own reflection,
   Swirling sweetness into ache;
And we—tiny alchemies of stardust—
Sip eternity through the straw of breath.

   So let each dawn drip again,
   Let the air taste of renewal;
For between each exhale and inhale
Lives the honey—ever golden, ever now.

*After After-Thoughts*

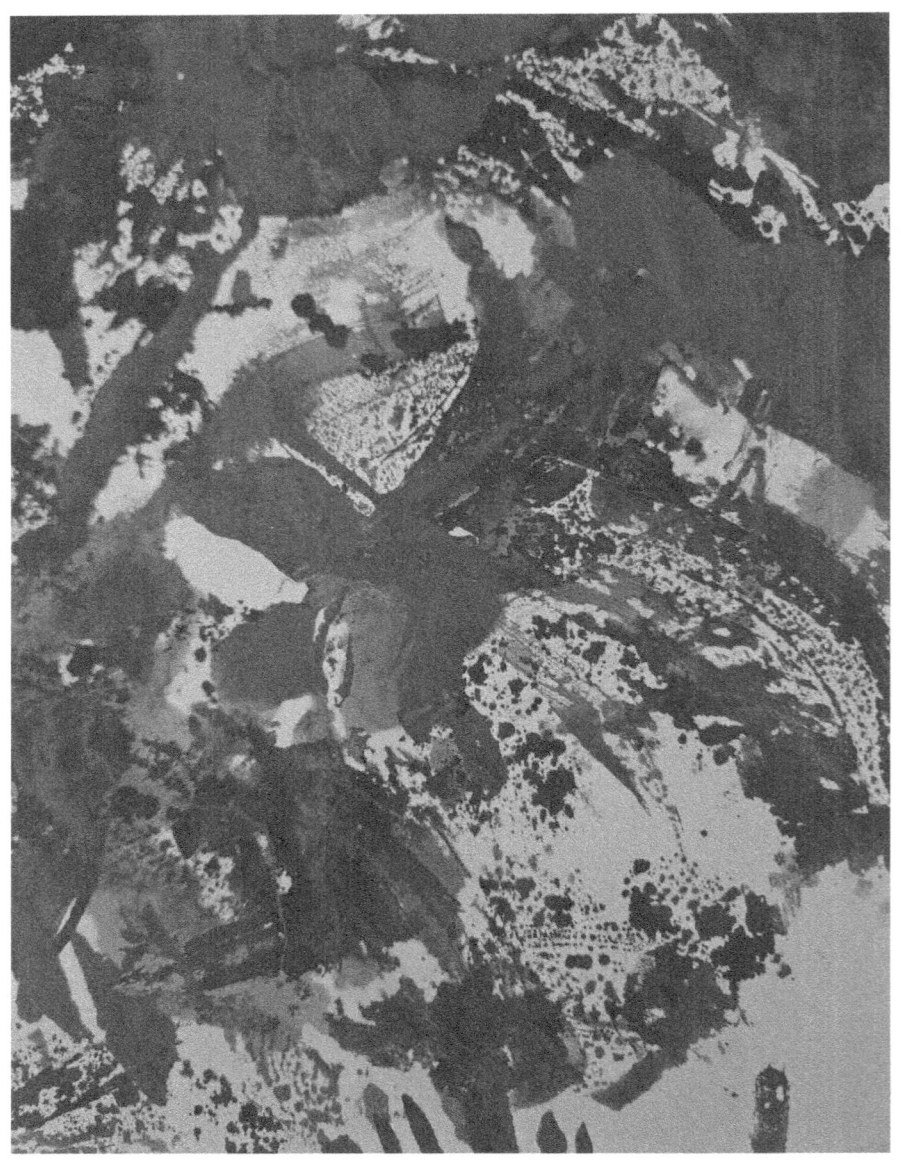

*After After-Thoughts*

# Fore First Drop

tender wakes matin born sun
groggy leas exhale their mist
for wispy white umbrellas

to glide on silent whispers
heralding green arrival

of white dandelions' roar

red swollen dewy tongues lust
to lick again Aura's smile
for stolen cotton pecks

with cheeks red, lashes flutter
the shy blushes abound, as
life anew betwixt her leaves

O, so sodden, nectar bleeds
till puckered lips are agleam

during afternoon showers
rivulets flood veiled boudoirs
a promised natural tryst
begins always with a kiss

dew pearls cling to slender stems
their tremble hums a low hymn
the meadow bends, half-asleep

soft zephyrs unclasp her gown
each blade glistens, newly shorn
breath of earth sighs through the corn

*After After-Thoughts*

a robin hums in hush tones
to wake the sleeping valley
each note falls like a soft tear

through the blue-veined canopy
light refracts in sugared arcs
sweet delirium, sky's mark

her bosom, emerald and moist
heaves beneath the warming hand
of some ancient lover's plan

the brook's murmur grows rapture
liquid tongues sip mossy beds
reeds quiver at the slightest glance

in shadows, two petals press
their scent mingling mid-air's drift
whispered vows no wind could lift

the forest's pulse quickens still
sap ascends in trembling thrill
like the first pulse after sleep

bees drunk on golden delight
stumble through the clover's hush
bodies hum the hymns of touch

and still, the sun's hot query
burns on each unbuttoned hill
time itself slows to a spill

moist breath turns the air tender
pollen floats like whispered prayer
each mote hung on threads of care

*After After-Thoughts*

a lover's sigh, soft thunder
stirs beneath the orchard bloom
fruit swells at the promise made

evening's breath, lavender gray
drips from the edge of the day
a hush blankets every bay

now, beneath the bowed willow
shadows curl like gentle arms
and cradle dusk's final charm

night's cool hand soothes each fever
as star-milk crowns every leaf
and silence hums belief

the moon, round-eyed and knowing
smiles upon their dewy sheen
time folds softly, evergreen

where fore first drop had fallen
still glistens her sacred sign—
a world reborn from the brine.

*After After-Thoughts*

# Missing Steps

Din of silence muffles pause between breaths
Every peal a rung – a first syllable
Of a moment exhausted and past
Primal words lacking exact

Unheard echoes ripple within bone
Meaning trembles before thought's edge
Speech unformed, still gesturing forward
Tongue tasting ghosts of intent

Steps forgotten by dusted corridors
Ankles remember what lips cannot
Sound trapped in the hush of before
Memory pacing an absent stair

Ceilings lean with patient gravity
Holding light in cracked reflections
Each ray folds its confession inward
Becoming stillness, becoming name

Windows ache beneath their own transparency
Outside bleeds into within
The eye blinks and erases distance
Vision devours what it means to see

Fingers trace the air's faint seam
A map of where touch once wandered
Every print evaporates mid-gesture
Like dew fearing the rise of reason

*After After-Thoughts*

The floor hums beneath thought's restraint
Echo of heel, pulse of purpose
Yet the body hesitates—
Half-mind, half-muscle, wholly between

Walls breathe in sync with the clock
Each tick a minor resurrection
Of what the hour never truly held
Only measured, then let dissolve

Dreams curl in the rafters
Whispering rehearsals of waking
Names fall like dust through the gaps
Unspoken syllables sleep in the light

The mouth opens—no sound arrives
Only the idea of a word
A sound before language,
A yearning before shape

Every silence rehearses return
Yet never performs it completely
Echo becomes rumor,
Rumor becomes rest

The page absorbs its own confession
Ink listening harder than sight
Meaning shifts under weightless grammar
As if thought refused translation

Clouds rearrange their unspoken syntax
Heaven drafts its own correction
Rain edits each forgotten vow
Until only reflection remains

*After After-Thoughts*

Hands recall their unfinished labor
Building scaffolds of invisible time
Each nail an argument with gravity
Each pause a truce with loss

The breath, a clock without hands
Tells of seconds that never agreed
To stay in sequence
Or to leave in peace

Steps erased still lead somewhere
Though not where they began
Absence constructs its own architecture
Where forgetting feels like faith

The horizon hums beneath closed eyes
Soundless, yet full of direction
Distance folds into the pupil
And vanishes without trace

The tongue remembers the shape of truth
But the mouth denies pronunciation
Language fractures at its root
Meaning waits in unfinished bloom

Rooms remain though walls recede
The body a whisper of furniture
Occupying what it cannot name
Dwelling in the absence of arrival

*After After-Thoughts*

Shadows keep their own counsel
They measure the soul by subtraction
Each darkness trimmed to fit memory
Each silence cut to size

Stillness grows like coral—
Minute, intricate, alive in hush
Every pause another reef of thought
Every sigh a living stone

The earth keeps its secrets in tremors
Listening to us from below
Our weight, our hesitation—
Translations of being into gravity

The last sound is almost a color
The first color, almost a cry
Both vanish where they meet
Between what was heard and meant

Silence inhales what time exhales
Leaving us mid-step, mid-word,
Balanced between absence and arrival—
Missing nothing but the next breath.

*After After-Thoughts*

*After After-Thoughts*

# Time Machine

Within babes eyes
Stars bridge edges
of the universe

Rhythms fortify
Every beat
Must your heart

Time suspends eternally
Life sentence—forever
Unshackled by chains

A primal scream,
An umbilical scab
Wombed memory

Faint, no longer
Floating in
Mother juice

Throat parched
Lactation ceased
Unjust deserts

On Earth
Soiled, awash
In years

Forever and never
For always
Before and after

*After After-Thoughts*

We wail!

Ashes inhale
Breath unmade
Dreams undone

Cradles dissolve
In twilight's palm
Eternity crawls

Every molecule
A witness sworn
To rebirth

The skin remembers
Fingers of galaxies
Braiding fate

From silence
A pulse stirs—
Ancient, relentless

Bones whisper
Through marrowed light
Echoing stars

Each cell prays
To its maker's hum
Unheard, eternal

Wind translates
What blood forgets
Into sky

*After After-Thoughts*

Love's fossil
Pressed beneath
Time's riverbed

We bloom again
In absence
Of reason

Gravity's kiss
Returns the child
To seed

Mother moon
Bends low
To listen

Father sun
Renews his vow
Of burning

Memory bleeds
Into the ether's mouth
Naming no one

The fetus dreams
Of afterlife
Before birth

We fall upward
Into yesterday's womb
Again and again

Time turns
Its invisible wheel
Within us

## My Familiar

Within my hand
I catch the wind
Fingering the face
In last night's dream
Less a breeze

Just out of view
One step ahead me
Entering a door
About to shut

Obscured, a broken eyelash

Shadowed

Reality plucked

Before a dawn break
Tomorrow's yesterday
Fades from memory

With a profiled grin

It waits

And sometimes whistles

Always laughing
From the reverse side
Of a two-way mirror

I trace the echo
Of that laughter's hush
Between the ticks
Of a clock
That forgot its hour

*After After-Thoughts*

A reflection shifts—
Is it me
Or what I left
When I woke
Too soon?

It hums my name
From the corner
Of a painting
I never finished

The pigment moves
Like breath
Inside the frame
And sighs again

A candle flickers
But no draft comes
Only the whisper
Of unspoken thought

Its face reforms
In the glass of tea
Rising
From cup to fog

How long have I known it—
This constant shimmer
Behind my eyes?

It knows my footsteps
Better than I
Counts them backward
Across wet stone

*After After-Thoughts*

In the hush
Of mid-thought pause
It settles
In the marrow
And hums lullabies

The air bends
Where it smiles
A distortion
Of what once
Felt solid

My shadow lags

Tethered

By invisible laughter

The dream returns
With another's voice
Borrowing mine
To say goodnight

A knock at the heart—
No door in sight
Yet hinges creak

I follow the scent
Of something burning
But find
Only light

Each breath now
Half belonging
To the unseen half

*After After-Thoughts*

*After After-Thoughts*

It teaches silence
By echoing sound
That never was

Rain against glass
Mimics its rhythm
Tap by tap

When I sleep again
It borrows my eyes
To look back
Through the mirror

It asks nothing
But leaves questions
Curled in the dark

I have learned
Not to answer

Yet every dawn

It greets me first

Before thought, before name

A presence clothed
In yesterday's air
That never leaves

It waits still—
The familiar
That remembers me
Better than I remember it

# One-Only-One II

**1**

Words from a fragmented heart
confuse unaccented vowels
with consonant periods
that dangle from a passive voice;
every clause turns
into a subject lacking a destination,
just a faulty point of view.

**2**

An emotional subject
is the phrase
"to be or not . . ."
a subjunctive mood
has a nominative run-on
with *I am,* as if it were indicative.

**3**

Syntax has been tense
since the day a once-betrothed
enunciated the declarative life sentence—
"I do."

**4**

Negation is lonely.
Now I don't.

**5**

Semicolons ache
between pauses too long for breath,
too brief for memory—
each mark a tiny grave
for what might have continued.

**6**
Parentheses cradle silence;
they hold what cannot be said
without disturbing
the fragile grammar of loss.

**7**
Every verb declines,
bent backward toward what was,
the infinitive of yearning
split by time.

**8**
Ellipses drift—
a hesitant sigh,
trailing off into unspoken thought
like lovers who stop mid-sentence.

**9**
Articles vanish.
There is no *the,*
no *a,*
only *absence.*

**10**
Apostrophes clutch possession,
but what is owned
escapes the page.

**11**
Capital letters shout
as if grief could be formalized
by rule or rubric,
but even uppercase sorrow
cannot begin a new line.

*After After-Thoughts*

**12**
Punctuation mourns—
periods like eyes closing,
colons like unfinished prayers.

**13**
Pronouns betray.
*We* becomes *you,*
then *I,*
then none.

**14**
Tenses shift—
present becomes preterit,
future conditional,
love subjunctive.

**15**
Every clause returns
to the clause before it,
a recursive lament
looping through loss.

**16**
Conjugation is confession:
I loved, I love, I will not—
each tense a smaller truth.

**17**
Even the prepositions flee,
leaving the sentence stranded
between *from* and *to*
with nowhere to go.

*After After-Thoughts*

**18**
Diacritics fade;
accent marks lose faith
in emphasis.

**19**
The lexicon thins
like aging paper—
each word a brittle petal
fallen from syntax.

**20**
In the margin,
a forgotten note still reads:
*rewrite the ending.*

**21**
But endings resist revision;
they are absolute,
like the sound of a closing parenthesis.

**22**
Between subject and object
hangs a ghost—
once predicate, now pause.

**23**
Meaning erodes
under the weight of commas
never placed,
breaths never taken.

*After After-Thoughts*

**24**

The grammar of grief
has no direct object.

**25**

And yet, a phrase survives:
"I might."
It flickers like a lowercase candle.

**26**

Somewhere, a conjunction waits
to reconnect two halves
of a severed sentence.

**27**

Hope hides in the footnotes—
annotated faintly in pencil:
*see also: forgiveness.*

28

So the page remains open,
the voice recursive,
a single pronoun whispering
through fractured syntax—
still trying to be
one-only-one.

*After After-Thoughts*

*After After-Thoughts*

# The Tattered-Tale Heart

kindling wisps
dance on musty air

her Winter kiss
swaddles me in
warm memories,

a cedared smoked sweater
with an overlooked
gravy stain,

membered moments

when embers glowed
as bright
as long
as smiles
from "Just one more
before I go"

another log
half- a- nog
extra nutmeg
dusted mustache
a tasty afterthought
till the next

"Goodnight"

when winds
blow me
beside
your comfy fire

*After After-Thoughts*

the clock coughs once
its chime a sigh
that echoes through
a room still full
of something left unsaid

the mug still warm
where lips once perched
awaits a hand
that doesn't reach

smoke curls upward
like a question
that never lands

its ghostly twine

wraps my breath

in cinnamon recollections

your laughter—
a flicker,
a spark that startles
then fades
into woolen hush

outside the pane
the frost rehearses
the patterns of
forgotten promises

inside,

each coal confesses

its slow undoing

*After After-Thoughts*

I stir them gently,
caretaker of
their final glow

how many nights
have whispered through
this heart's forgiving throat?

how many winters
have I borrowed
to keep your scent

from leaving?

a single thread
of smoke recalls
the sleeve you tugged
when laughter caught us both
off guard

and even now
the chair across
seems weighted still
with you

the shadow there—
a stubborn guest
who will not leave
though time insists

I close my eyes,
and hear the crack—
not wood, but heart—
in steady syncopation

flame-light fingers
trace the wall,
spelling out
our quiet coda

*After After-Thoughts*

a love
half-wrapped in wool
half-burning still

a matchstick thought
ignites again
the tender scene
of snowflakes dancing
on your lashes

I reach for warmth
but find only
the echo of your hum
against the grate

even ashes glow
if memory wills it

so I will tend

this fading fire

till morning's pale reprieve

for somewhere
in the smoke's ascent
your name
still curls
and lingers there—

a tattered-tale heart
that will not rest
until
the last spark
flames our moments
again.

*After After-Thoughts*

*After After-Thoughts*

# A Nutmeg Kiss

a smidgen early
you may think,
but, tonight
nipping Winter winds
kissed the last
of Summer's warmth
from my cheeks.

yes—fading pages
turning faster
than yellowed memories
of crooked smiles
from jack-o'-lanterns
carved standing
on a highchair

while pumpkin pies
browned before dinner
and grace was sung
as we held hands
and felt
our hearts
beat as though
they were
always One.

and in that hush
before dessert,
where nutmeg lingered
in the air's embrace,

*After After-Thoughts*

I saw your eyes
reflecting embers—
a quiet knowing
that seasons pass
but love does not.

outside, the trees
bent low in prayer,
their brittle leaves
confessing light's retreat;
yet in our kitchen's glow,
the candles swayed
like souls remembering
that warmth can bloom
even after frost.

so let the wind
claim what it will—
we'll keep the scent
of sugar and spice,
the echo of laughter,
and the grace
of our small forever,
tucked inside
the turning year.

*After After-Thoughts*

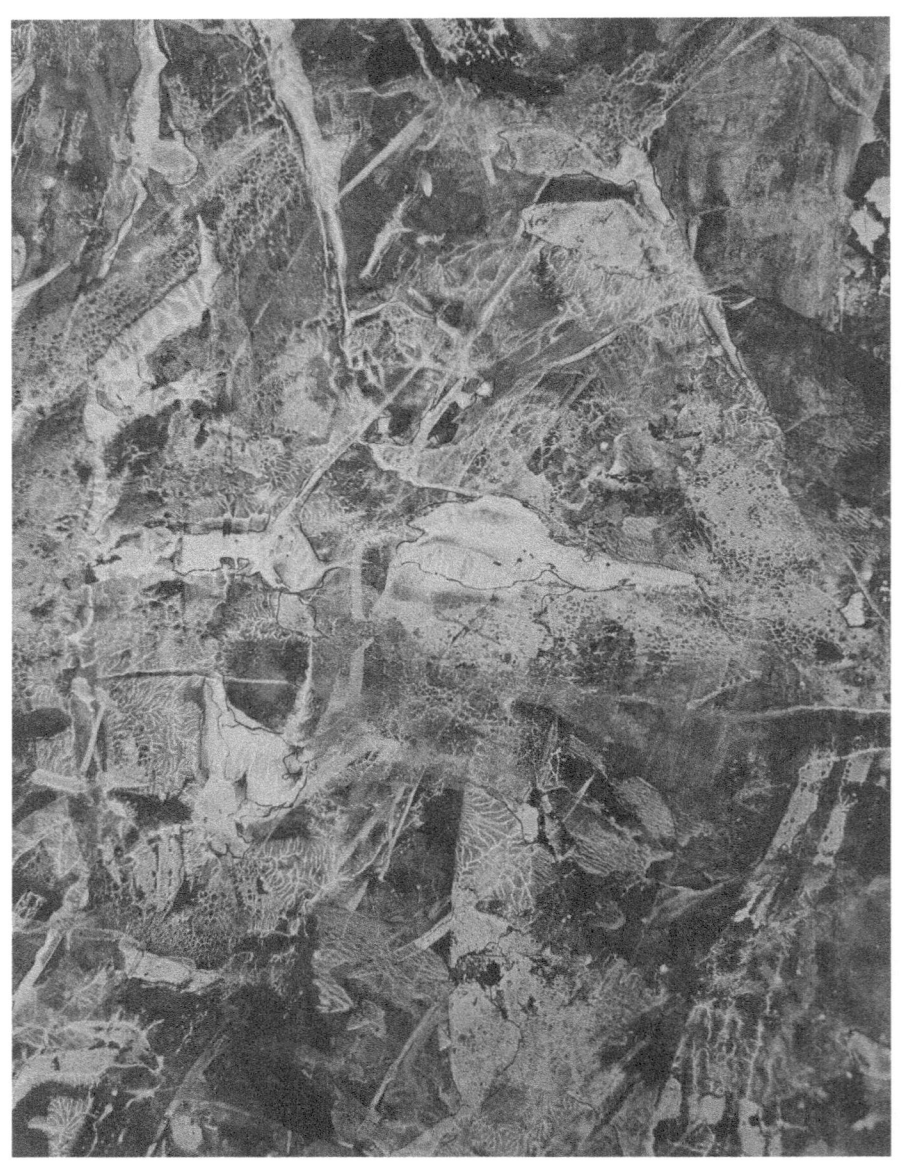

## Home in Loam

spring bulbs
sleep
in silent umbra
by redbreast

first chirp,
gelid rivulets

seep on

palettes—
painting furrows
for crocus clawing
loamy thaw
to unfurl
salverform array;
naked sylphs,
holding hands,
lift their heads

and bask
in matin sun

dew trembles
on furred stems,
translucent pearls
of thawing grief—
each drop remembers
winter's ache,
each spark renews
the art of faith.

*After After-Thoughts*

worms stir
beneath the hush,
twisting scripture
in the soil,
penning psalms
to fertile gods
of rot and bloom.

trowels sleep
in leaning sheds,
rusted edges
dream of use—
while fingers,
dirty yet divine,
crumble frost
to cradle life.

wind murmurs
through thawed hedges,
a psalm of patience,
a hymn of wait—
how quietly
the world begins
again.

moss awakens
on stone altars,
green tongues
licking frost away;
lichen sigils
reclaim faith
from walls once numb.

*After After-Thoughts*

brittle reeds
whisper beside
the vernal creek—
their rustling voices
rise like incense,
holy smoke
to April's dawn.

anemone eyes
blink open,
startled by
their own color—
a painter's prayer
in violet syllables.

snails sermonize
in spiraled shells,
bearing the world
on their damp backs;
they write slow gospels
in the mud.

the robin bows,
listening—
to roots confess
beneath its feet,
to seedling sins
and promises
in green tongues.

mud-slick knees
of kneeling gardeners
press against
the pulse of March;
they pray in touch,
not words.

*After After-Thoughts*

fingers dig
where faith begins—
under frost,
under doubt—
and lift the tender,
threaded heart
of spring.

from furrows
breath rises—
an unseen hymn
to the sun god
returning.

earth hums,
low and steady,
a note of mercy
beneath each step;
sap answers,
flowing upward,
a chant of resurrection.

rooks gather
in bare branches,
scribes of dusk
and thaw;
their black robes
flutter with
unwritten verses.

spades glint,
baptized in meltwater,
as if
steel too
longed to bloom.

*After After-Thoughts*

hands become
icons of toil—
creased, cracked,
earth-creased,
yet holy
in their stain.

every nail
a crescent moon
of loam,
each palm
a palette
of resurrection.

under every fingernail,
a tiny cosmos
spins—
root and rot,
hope and humus,
the quiet mathematics
of growth.

the sun leans
through mist,
a lantern hung
in breath;
the field listens
to its slow ascent.

a child's laughter
skips through thaw,
melting even
the elder snow—
renewal wears
a smaller face
each year.

*After After-Thoughts*

petals pulse
in patient throats;
buds hold secrets
tighter than prayer beads—
and still they open.

a robin plucks
a thread of worm,
offering communion
to the dawn;
the altar hums
with humble grace.

the gardener wipes
sweat and soil
across his cheek—
a smudge of creation
no sermon
could replace.

the bulbs stretch,
drinking memory,
exhaling light;
each stem
an echo
of divine repetition.

breezes braid
the scent of thaw
into hymns;
their chorus carries
through quiet limbs
of birch and bone.

*After After-Thoughts*

tiny stones
gleam like promises
beneath the tilled earth;
each one
a heart once cold,
now keeping warmth.

beneath all that grows,
the silence roots deeper—
dark, eternal,
a mother's hum
cradling every color
yet to rise.

dirt collects
under love's hands,
not shame;
each streak of earth
a testament
to touch.

clouds wander
like thoughts
of an older god—
forgiving,
forgetting,

beginning again.
a tulip speaks
in scarlet vowels,
its breath
a new alphabet
of grace.

*After After-Thoughts*

the robin returns—
song heavier now,
but truer,
richer
for the waiting.

every bulb
that breaks
the dark
says the same thing:
thank you.

and the earth,
in kind,
answers softly—
you're welcome.

*After After-Thoughts*

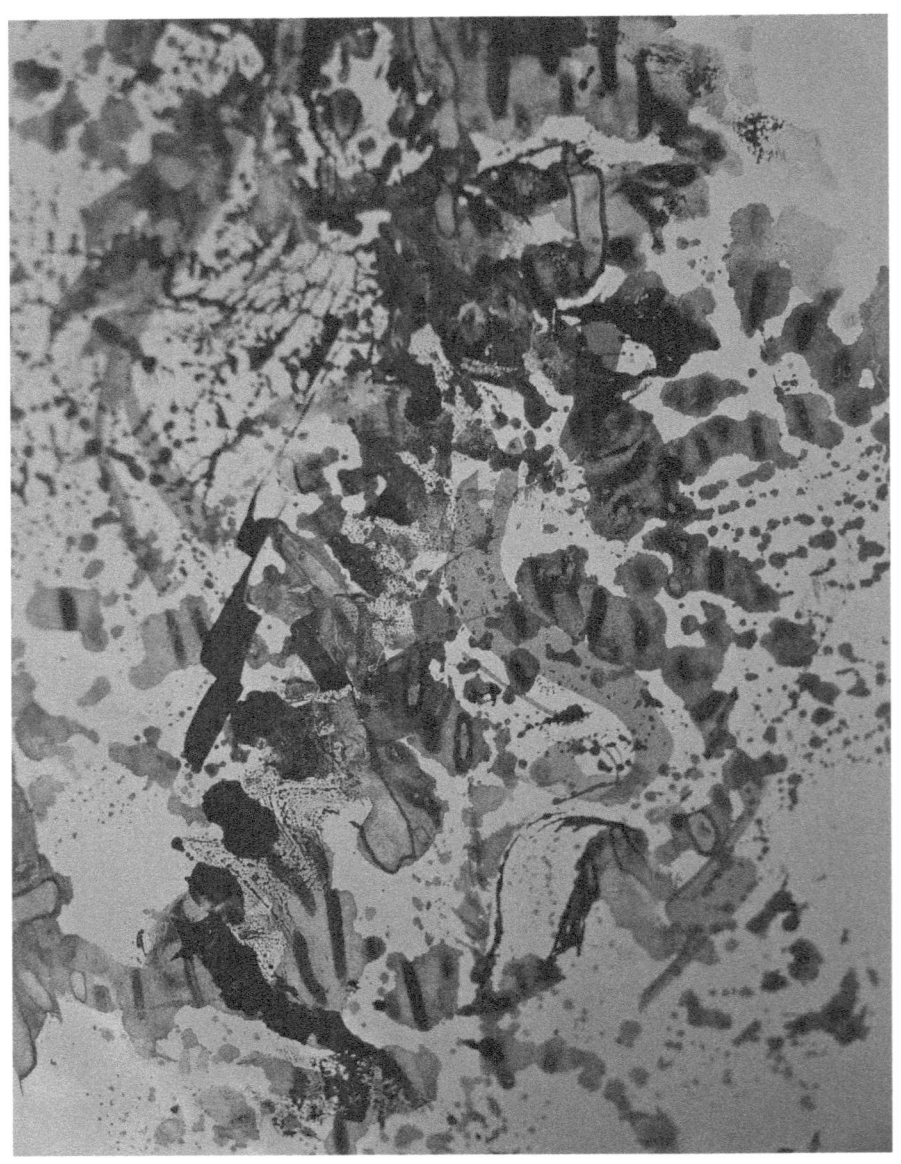

# Curling Fingers

early breeze,
feather wisp,
intention fills
memory's
vacant white seat

odors forge
flameless candles,
every new light,
count the years,
pass to past

fading moon
in autumn,
crusty inclines
crumble fast,
attention wane

jelled gray matter
now shadow shot,
withered fingers
pinch another
life-story pleat

pulse hums faint,
through wrist-veins
woven tight
like reeds
that hum in wind

ink dries slow,
on trembling page,
each blot
a name once whispered
soft to dusk

*After After-Thoughts*

clocks lean forward,
their faces cracked—
time's grin
shows missing teeth,
still it ticks.

eyelids flutter,
moth-light thin,
seeking flame
that once was
unafraid of dark.

dust in the corner
forms small cathedrals,
each mote
a psalm
for lost recall.

chairs remember
knees that bent,
weight that prayed
for strength,
for grace, for more.

windows ache
with seeing too long—
rain leaves
streaked elegies
across their skin.

the kettle hums
a ghostly song,
steam rising,
like unfinished thoughts
from lips gone still.

*After After-Thoughts*

books exhale
their patient dust,
spines cracked
where wisdom slept
too long unread.

footsteps echo
in carpet's nap,
soft indentations—
a history
of brief returns.

photographs
blur their borders,
eyes once vivid
now fog
in silver haze.

mirrors blink,
reluctant glass,
forgetting faces
that once demanded
to be seen.

the house breathes slow,
walls expand
then contract—
old lungs
of plaster and paint.

shadows learn
to speak again,
mimicking laughter
of those who
no longer call.

*After After-Thoughts*

somewhere,
a curtain stirs—
no wind,
just the memory
of movement.

hands unclasp,
air takes hold,
a final furling
like petals
after storm.

silence folds
into deeper folds,
a blanket
drawn over
the voice of clocks.

dreams collect
in corners now,
needing neither
door nor dawn
to enter.

moon returns,
less sure this time,
dimly tracing
what's left
of reflection.

breath grows pale,
a leaf's surrender—
the body listening
to itself
let go.

*After After-Thoughts*

and yet—
some pulse persists,
a whisper
beneath the dust,
soft as intent.

perhaps tomorrow
unfurls again,
a thought reborn
through fingers
learning light.

*After After-Thoughts*

# Rays of a Son

Rays of the sun
Glimmers of Futures Past
Sparkling fragments of gemstones
adorning crowns worn during times
when blue oceans shimmered with barges

deep to water-lines, with brimming clay vessels,
filled with fragrant oils and tangy spices
from lands below the horizon,
cover my feet.

They are but vestiges collecting between my toes,
in search of memories, flowing from those
who waded in these friendly waters
that lap against the very rocks,
where one day I hope to sit
and turn my grain of sand
between these thirsty fingers.

The wind hums a low refrain
as if it remembers the names
of ships that never returned,
of sailors who whispered to the moon
their promises of return.

Each grain glows briefly,
a word, a tear, a wish,
echoing through the hollow shell
of my hand cupped to the tide.

*After After-Thoughts*

I hear the laughter of merchants,
coins clinking in sunlit tongues,
children chasing shadows of gulls,
their joy spilled like light
across the wet shore.

The sea folds their laughter away,
layer by layer, beneath the drift—
a library of salt and silence
bound in coral and foam.

Even now, I taste the ancient trade,
sweet citrus and sandalwood,
wine and honey aging in barrels
carved by unseen hands.

A breeze carries a scent of myrrh—
a ghost of the desert crossing,
camel bells fading into rhythm
with the surf's eternal prayer.

My feet sink deeper into stories
no longer spoken aloud,
only dreamed in murmurs
beneath sleeping waves.

A shell presses against my heel—
its spiral, a cipher of beginnings,
of voices drawn inward,
retelling birth and departure
without ever ceasing.

*After After-Thoughts*

Somewhere beyond sight,
the horizon exhales light,
a boundary that is never fixed
but sways like memory in water.

And I recall a mother's touch,
cool as river stones,
her song drifting with the tide—
a melody of shelter and surrender.

The sun leans lower,
painting my shadow in gold,
its warmth an inheritance
passed from star to skin.

My reflection trembles,
broken into fragments—
a mosaic of selves
that once believed in permanence.

Evening folds the sky into silk.
The sea becomes a mirror of dusk,
holding both the living and the lost
in equal measure.

I bend and lift a pebble—
it pulses faintly with memory,
a fossil of breath and longing
smoothed by centuries of return.

If I listen closely,
I hear the rustle of tomorrow,
soft as a promise
not yet spoken aloud.

*After After-Thoughts*

Light spills like confession
across the shore's open palm,
and for a moment,
the world forgets its weight.

Time loosens its tether,
flowing back toward the source,
where every ripple began
with a single trembling hand.

The tide climbs higher,
a gentle insistence,
urging me toward surrender,
toward the quiet inside the wave.

Stars will inherit this place soon,
their silver glances winking
between the reeds,
blessing what remains unseen.

And I,
small as a whisper in sand,
turn once more my grain between my fingers—
a sunbeam held captive,
a life in miniature,
a glimmer of futures past.

*After After-Thoughts*

# Fires of Mt. Erato

Just before morning
it erupted
in one long moment.

Isolation devastated
by the blast,
pillows crushed
into hillocks,
posts forged inside walls.

Clouds billowed
of white satin,
sheeting victims below
in particles of hot ash,
pumicing their skin
to a glisten.

In the heat
magma pushed
continents into
a single rock
of contentment.

Lava spoke
in tongues of honey,
its syllables dripping
onto lips
that trembled
with new geography.

*After After-Thoughts*

Crimson rivers
ran over
the plains of reason,
melting boundaries
once cold as sleep.

Bodies turned
to monuments,
each curve
a remnant
of worship and ruin.

Desire hissed
through fissures,
sulfur tasting
like the truth after prayer.

The mountain sighed,
its breath perfumed
with longing's smoke—
a hymn for those
who dared to linger.

Ash settled
in the silence,
veiling the earth
like mourning cloth
for lost restraint.

Even the birds
forgot direction,
their wings
beating shadows
into surrender.

*After After-Thoughts*

The sea watched,
boiling with envy,
throwing salt
onto tongues
that called her name.

From the crater's core
a whisper rose,
soft as silk
and sharp as flame—
*Remember me.*

Night returned,
but dimmer now,
as though stars
had witnessed too much
and could not speak.

Roots glowed beneath,
drawing fire
into their veins,
teaching trees
to dream of thunder.

Villages slept
under blankets of glass,
translucent memories
of love
once molten.

## After After-Thoughts

The moon hid her face,
ashamed of her pallor,
while Venus blushed
a shade too deep
for dawn to bear.

Hands reached
from cooled stone,
still clasping
what could not
be cooled within.

A god's laughter
echoed in crevices,
mocking mortals
for mistaking
heat for grace.

When wind returned,
it carried fragments—
songs of touch,
breath, and ruin—
stitched by time's own needle.

The fields turned fertile
with remembered fire,
seeds igniting
in the hush
of regeneration.

And lovers came
centuries later,
walking barefoot
on the scar,
feeling it pulse.

*After After-Thoughts*

They kissed,
and for an instant
the mountain stirred,
as if dreaming
of rebirth.

Just before morning
again it trembled—
not from fury,
but from memory's
eternal desire.

## After After-Thoughts

*After After-Thoughts*

# No Help Wanted

Ignore my
click-clack
you need not
sneak a peek;
blindness fingers
the fear,
silence says
you're there.

An electric chair
sits before you;
pity shackles
well meant feats.

The warning missives
H-a-n-d-i-c-a-p
the apologies
never cease.

"There but
by the grace
of God
go I,"
you say
under your breath.

Shaking hands
with guilt
is all
the sickness
you get.

*After After-Thoughts*

Do not hold
the door—
it opens
both ways.

Do not speak
slowly,
my ears
are not
on strike.

Your kindness
is a cage
with velvet bars.

The stairs
are not
Mount Everest—
just stone
and gravity.

Let me fall
if fall
I must—
that's how
we learn
to stand.

Your glance
burns holes
through courage's
thin cloth.

I am not
your mirror
for mercy.

*After After-Thoughts*

Your prayer
slips like oil
down my spine.

My cane
is not
a cross.

I rise
each morning
uncrucified,
though the nails
are waiting.

There's a map
beneath this skin—
lines of pain
and practice.

Do not trace it
with sympathy's
finger.

Touch it
only if
you dare
to see yourself.

The chair rolls
but I steer.
Your push
tips the balance
too far.

Your whisper
of bravery
turns courage
into currency.

*After After-Thoughts*

Keep your coins—
I've paid
in full.

Do not say
"I understand."
You don't.
You shouldn't.
And that's
alright.

I do not ask
for pity's prayer,
only space
to breathe
my own air.

Your eyes
search for broken,
but find
unfinished.

Your words
search for healing,
but find
being.

Your heart
searches for giving—
mine
for grace
to refuse.

*After After-Thoughts*

Still,
sometimes,
your silence
feels
like kindness.

A nod,
a passing glance,
a rhythm
without apology.

That is
enough.

That
is help
not wanted—
but received.

*After After-Thoughts*

*After After-Thoughts*

# Past Event Horizons

Spiraling circles form all,
fragments picked up along the way,
multi-colored sparkles sojourn on timelines
while what-ifs wait to be born.

Never ending, a perfect beginning,
nothingness full of potential.
One begins an infinity
with a BANG.

Before light remembered itself,
darkness hummed a lullaby of ions.
Matter married energy,
and their children became motion.

Each spark carried a secret—
a whisper from unmeasured time.
Gravity bent its knee,
courting dust to dance.

Galaxies twirled like thought-forms,
naming themselves through rotation.
Color arrived late—
an afterthought of longing.

Somewhere between mass and dream,
you opened your eyes.
Memories drifted backward,
searching for ancestors not yet born.

*After After-Thoughts*

Comets rehearsed their arcs,
like pen strokes before a signature.
Every collision composed a chord,
every silence its echo.

Atoms leaned into each other,
forgetting how to be alone.
Light wove through them,
a needle threading purpose.

In the quiet fabric of space,
time exhaled its first breath.
Moments unfolded like petals,
refusing to stop blooming.

Infinity rehearsed itself in mirrors,
each reflection slightly late.
What is origin but repetition
wearing a new face?

The pulse that began the cosmos
beats still beneath your ribs.
Dreams carry fossils of the first explosion—
glowing phosphenes beneath the eyelids.

Love is the universe remembering
it once was whole.
Loss, the echo of expansion—
distance made visible.

Planets hum hymns in elliptical prayer,
each orbit a vow renewed.
Entropy kneels,
then rises as creation's twin.

*After After-Thoughts*

The edge of time curls inward,
folding light into shadow's pocket.
We are photons slowed by fear,
learning again to move.

Across every horizon,
event becomes memory, memory dream.
The spiral widens,
and still it is a circle.

Somewhere, another beginning waits,
already remembering us.
And in that instant—
nothingness full of potential.

*After After-Thoughts*

*After After-Thoughts*

# Walking on Water

In summer,
the Chesapeake Bay sun
fries me
pancake brown.
Sweat pours
like maple syrup

held by
tiny hands,
that will one day

skip worn stones
over ebbing waves,
where on

floating paths
I'll lightly step
onto orange blossoms
with scents of all
tomorrows
past.

The pier groans
beneath my bare feet,
salt and cedar
mingling in air
like two prayers
sharing one tongue.

A crab boat coughs
in the distance,
its wake
spelling my name
in cursive foam,
erased before noon.

*After After-Thoughts*

Pelicans dive
with priestly grace,
breaking the hush
of heat and hymn.
Each splash
a sermon on faith.

Marsh grass whispers
in secret codes,
the tide translating
only for those
who still remember
childhood's hush.

I breathe in
the rot of life,
sweet and sour
as ripened memory—
the Bay forgiving
its own decay.

A jellyfish blooms
beneath the pier,
a ghostly lantern
rising slow,
its pulse
a metronome of time.

Somewhere inland,
thunder rolls—
soft as a mother's
low warning.
I smile,
already drenched.

*After After-Thoughts*

The water accepts
each step I take,
hesitant, holy—
an old trick
the heart relearns
after sorrow.

Evening leans
on the horizon's arm,
the sky tasting
of copper and rain.
Seagulls argue
like prophets.

My shadow folds
into the current,
a dark twin
unburdened by years—
its laughter
bubbling to the top.

Stars prick through
like seeds of light,
planted in the black loam
of night's surface.
The moon,
a silver oar.

I walk home
on reflected stars,
each ripple
a soft applause.
No miracles now—
just water, remembering.

*After After-Thoughts*

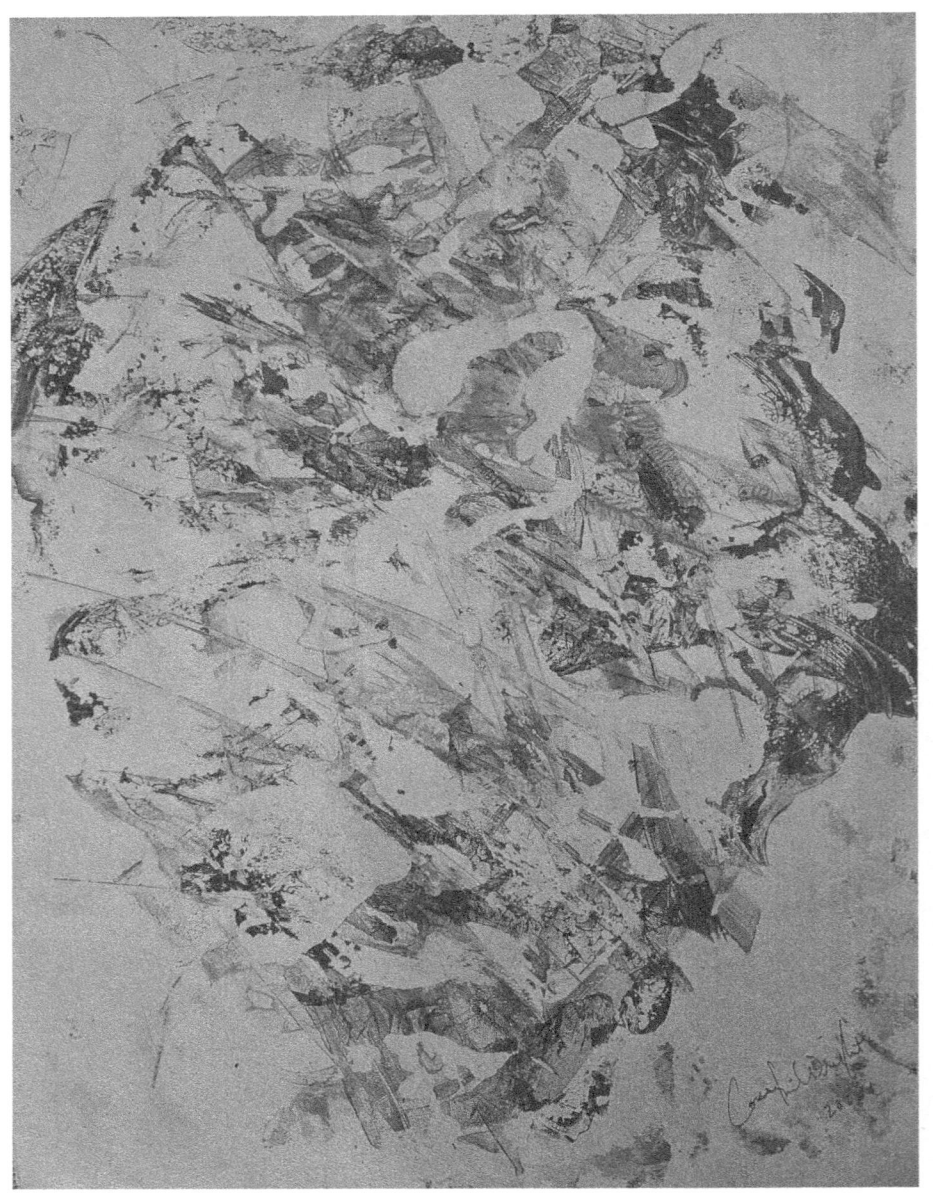

*After After-Thoughts*

# Your Bad

words
you
should
have

did
not

say

a

thing

*After After-Thoughts*

# Early in the City

Fifth Avenue walks
remind me

who am I

a bashful glance

stitch less mannequin
without a smile

chair for sale
seat of imagination

sleeper in doorway
dreaming inside a dream
bound in a numb shell
brown bag bottle doth runneth over

gray cloud overhead
filled with tears

no umbrella
cheeks wet at last

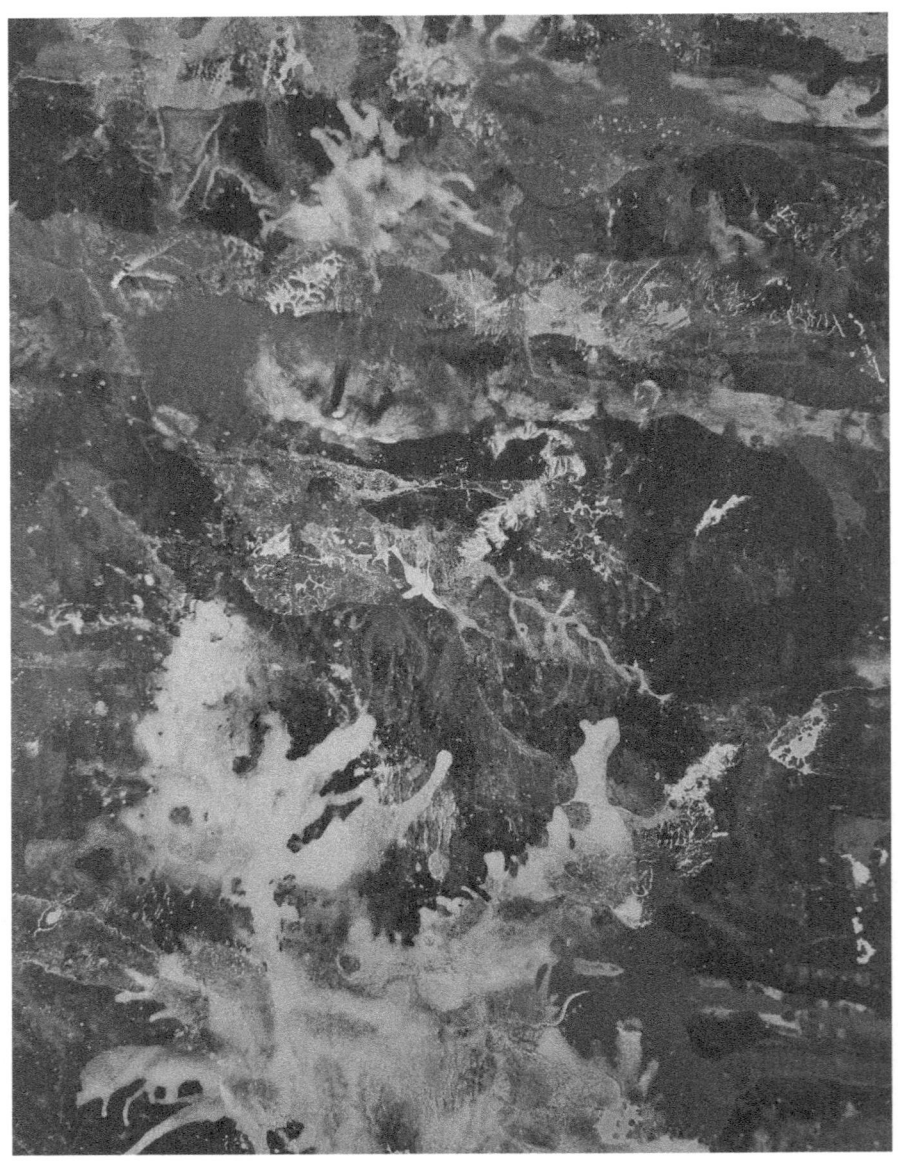

## A Cheap Vacation

dusty tomes
with destinations
unbound
book passages
on gossamer yachts.

Puffy white sails
float to lands
where dreams wait
on pages unturned;

imagining breezes
the only fare.

your return trip
is always guaranteed
in staterooms
with portals
looking
outside
what is
inside your mind.

the captain
knows no ports,
only tides
of thought
and memory's
shifting charts.

*After After-Thoughts*

each word
an oar
dipping
into oceans
of imagination—
no compass,
no crew.

paragraphs unfold
like shorelines
seen through fog,
sentences
curling back
to where they began.

a bookmark
becomes an anchor,
the spine
a mast
splitting
clouds of reverie.

in these cabins
light is borrowed
from some
forgotten noon;
ink the currency
of every crossing.

passengers whisper
in margins,
their stories
half erased
by salt
and sleep.

*After After-Thoughts*

      the storm
     is only paper
      wrinkling
with too much touch,
too much longing
   for elsewhere.

  when you dock,
you leave nothing—
only fingerprints
  on the cover,
  a faint scent
    of travel.

      still,
the voyage continues—
a tide of thought
folding inward,
where the horizon
meets the page.

and closing the book,
you find yourself
washed ashore
in your own
quiet room—
home again,
for free.

www.ingramcontent.com/pod-product-compliance
Lightning Source LLC
Chambersburg PA
CBHW032135040426
42449CB00005B/252